TEXAS TEST PREP

Writing Skills Quiz Book

STAAR Writing

Grade 3

ISBN 978-1481114233

CONTENTS

INTRODUCTION
For Parents, Teachers, and Tutors

About the Book

This book is focused on developing the student's writing skills. The first section develops editing and revising skills by giving students practice correcting and improving passages. The second section develops the language, vocabulary, and grammar skills that grade 3 students are expected to have.

STAAR Writing Test Preparation

The STAAR Writing test taken by grade 4 students contains several passages. Students read each passage and then answer questions about how to correct or improve the passage. Section 1 of this book gives students practice answering these types of questions. Section 2 of this book develops the specific skills that students need to answer these questions.

Section 1: Revising and Editing Quizzes

Section 1 of this book focuses on editing and revising. It contains 4 sets of 5 passages. Each passage is followed by a question set.

This section of the book contains passages and question sets similar to those on the STAAR Writing test, but shorter. The questions are just like those found on the STAAR Writing test and cover all the same skills. By completing this section, students will develop the writing skills they need to perform well on the state test, become familiar with the question types on the state test, and gain experience completing revising and editing tasks. Students will then be prepared and ready for the STAAR Writing test.

Section 2: Language, Vocabulary, and Grammar Quizzes

Section 2 of this book contains individual quizzes focused on each of the language skills that students need. These skills are described in the Texas curriculum known as the TEKS.

This section has 28 quizzes that cover the key skills described in the TEKS. By focusing on each skill individually, students will gain a full understanding of the skill. This understanding will help students perform well on the editing and revising sections of the STAAR Writing test. It will also improve reading comprehension and language skills, which will help students perform well in class and on the STAAR Reading tests.

Section 1
Revising and Editing Quizzes

Revising and Editing Quizzes

Set 1

Instructions

Read each passage. Each passage is followed by questions.

For each multiple-choice question, read the question carefully. Then select the best answer. Fill in the circle for the correct answer.

For other types of questions, follow the instructions given.

Building Your Vocabulary

As you read the passages, list any words you do not understand below. Use a dictionary to look up the meaning of the word. Write the meaning of the word below.

Word: _____

Meaning: _____

_____

Word: _____

Meaning: _____

_____

Word: _____

Meaning: _____

_____

Word: _____

Meaning: _____

_____

Word: _____

Meaning: _____

_____

Quiz 1

Read the passage below. Then answer the questions that follow it.

A Close Match

Anna and Juanita took their places on the court. The ball began to fly and bounce off they're rackets. The crowd turned their heads back and forth. Anna's friend Beth cheered each time she scored a point. Juanita's coach Demi cheered each time Juanita won a point. Juanita finally won the game.

After the game was over, Juanita walked to the middle of the net. About the loss, Anna was quite upset. She really wanted to storm off the court. But she knew that it wasn't the right thing to do. She met Juanita at the net.

"Good game," she said, as she shaked Juanita's hand.

"You too," Juanita said. "You made it a tough match to win."

Anna still felt a little upset. But she was proud of her for doing the right thing.

© Kent Mercurio

1   What is the best way to rewrite the sentence below?

   About the loss, Anna was quite upset.

   Ⓐ   About the loss quite upset, Anna was.

   Ⓑ   Anna was about the loss quite upset.

   Ⓒ   Anna was quite upset about the loss.

   Ⓓ   The loss, Anna was quite upset about.

2   Which word should replace *her* in the last sentence?

Ⓐ   she

Ⓑ   I

Ⓒ   me

Ⓓ   herself

3   Which word should replace the word *shaked* in the sentence below?

"Good game," she said, as she shaked Juanita's hand.

Ⓐ   shake

Ⓑ   shaking

Ⓒ   shook

Ⓓ   shooked

4   Which change should be made in the first paragraph?

Ⓐ   Change *began* to *begun*

Ⓑ   Change *they're* to *their*

Ⓒ   Change *scored* to *scoring*

Ⓓ   There is no change needed.

5   The passage states that Anna "wanted to storm off the court." This means that Anna wanted to —

Ⓐ   walk off in anger

Ⓑ   hide

Ⓒ   hurt Juanita

Ⓓ   win next time

Quiz 2

Read the passage below. Then answer the questions that follow it.

Polar Bears

Polar bears are large white bears that live in the arctic. Their main diet consists of seals or large animals that wash up onto the shore. Because of the fat they eat from these creatures, there is rare a need for the polar bear to drink water. This means that polar bears can survive on food alone. A polar bear eats an averrage of two kilograms of food per day. Thats like eating 20 to 30 burgers a day!

1   Place the following words from the passage in alphabetical order.

seals   survive   shore

_____   _____   _____

bears   burgers   because

_____   _____   _____

large   live   like

_____   _____   _____

2   Which word from the passage should start with a capital letter?

Ⓐ   large

Ⓑ   arctic

Ⓒ   shore

Ⓓ   kilograms

3   Which word should replace the word *rare* in the sentence below?

Because of the fat they eat from these creatures, there is rare a need for the polar bear to drink water.

Ⓐ   rarer

Ⓑ   rarely

Ⓒ   rareness

Ⓓ   rarest

4   What is the correct way to spell *averrage*?

Ⓐ   avrage

Ⓑ   avirage

Ⓒ   average

Ⓓ   avverage

5   Which change should be made in the passage?

Ⓐ   Change *shore* to *sure*

Ⓑ   Change *alone* to *allone*

Ⓒ   Change *Thats* to *That's*

Ⓓ   There is no change needed.

Quiz 3

Read the passage below. Then answer the questions that follow it.

Busy Bees

There are twenty thousend known species of bees in the world. Different types of honey bees make up only seven of those species. The honey bee is believed to have come from asia. However, scientists think that some species could have come from Europe. Bee stings can be very painful. Today, honey bees are used to help pollinate crops of flowers. They are also used to make honey and used to make beeswax.

Bees feed on the nectar and pollen found in flowers. As they move from flower to flower, they spread the pollen. This process pollinates flowers.

1   Identify three verbs and three nouns included in the sentences in the box above. Write the verbs and nouns in the table below.

Verbs	Nouns

2   Which word from the passage should start with a capital letter?

Ⓐ   species

Ⓑ   asia

Ⓒ   crops

Ⓓ   flowers

3   Which word from the passage is spelled incorrectly?

Ⓐ   thousend

Ⓑ   known

Ⓒ   different

Ⓓ   believed

4   What is the best way to rewrite the last sentence?

Ⓐ   They are also used to make honey, beeswax.

Ⓑ   They are also used to make honey and make beeswax.

Ⓒ   They are also used to make honey and beeswax.

Ⓓ   They are also used to make honey, make beeswax.

5   Which sentence does NOT belong in the passage?

Ⓐ   *Different types of honey bees make up only seven of those species.*

Ⓑ   *However, scientists think that some species could have come from Europe.*

Ⓒ   *Bee stings can be very painful.*

Ⓓ   *Today, honey bees are used to help pollinate crops of flowers.*

Quiz 4

Read the passage below. Then answer the questions that follow it.

Scrambled Eggs

Let's make some yummy scrambled eggs! There are six steps to making the perfect scrambled eggs. Let's do it:

1. First, crack two eggs into a saucepan.
2. Add 1 teaspoon of butter and a splash of milk.
3. Turn on the hotplate. You should ask an adult to turn on the hotplate for you.
4. Use a wooden spoon to scramble the eggs and burst the yolks.
5. Keep mixing as the eggs cook. The eggs will be ready when they are know longer runny. They will have a light and fluffy finish.
6. Add some salt and a little bit of pepper. Your eggs are ready to being enjoyed!

1   Circle all the words that are compound words.

yummy	scrambled	perfect
saucepan	teaspoon	butter
hotplate	wooden	mixing
finish	pepper	enjoyed

2   Which word in step 1 is a verb?

Ⓐ   crack

Ⓑ   two

Ⓒ   eggs

Ⓓ   saucepan

3   Which sentence could best be added to the first paragraph?

Ⓐ   Eggs are a good source of protein.

Ⓑ   Eggs can be used in breakfasts, dinners, and desserts.

Ⓒ   Scrambled eggs are quick and easy to make.

Ⓓ   I like to make scrambled eggs for my family.

4   What is the correct way to write the last sentence?

Ⓐ   Your eggs are ready to be enjoyed!

Ⓑ   Your eggs are ready to been enjoyed!

Ⓒ   Your eggs are ready being enjoyed!

Ⓓ   Your eggs are ready be enjoyed!

5   Which change should be made in step 5?

Ⓐ   Change *eggs* to *egg's*

Ⓑ   Change *have* to *had*

Ⓒ   Change *know* to *no*

Ⓓ   There is no change needed.

Quiz 5

Read the passage below. Then answer the questions that follow it.

Crash Landing

May 9 2012

Dear Annie,

Today I fell off my bike. I was going too fast along a rough track. At first, I began to cry. I was worried my bike was broked. Dad looked at it. He said it was okay, and that I should be more careful. He made me sit down for a little while to make sure I was alright. But I knew I was fine because falling off didn't even hurt! After a little while, I wanted to go and ride my bike again. It's times like these that I'm glad Dad makes me put on a helmet and knee guards!

Please write back soon. I can't wait to hear about your vacation.

Later,

Stacey

1   In the passage, the author uses contractions. A contraction is a shortened form of two words. Write the long form of each of the contractions below.

didn't   _____

It's   _____

I'm   _____

can't   _____

2   Which word rhymes with *rough*?

   Ⓐ   laugh

   Ⓑ   cough

   Ⓒ   stuff

   Ⓓ   safe

3   Which word should replace the word *broked* in the sentence below?

I was worried my bike was broked.

   Ⓐ   broke

   Ⓑ   broken

   Ⓒ   break

   Ⓓ   breaked

4   Which word should replace *and* in the sentence below?

He said it was okay, and that I should be more careful.

   Ⓐ   so

   Ⓑ   yet

   Ⓒ   or

   Ⓓ   but

5   What is the correct way to write the date at the start of the letter?

   Ⓐ   May, 9 2012

   Ⓑ   May 9, 2012

   Ⓒ   May, 9, 2012

   Ⓓ   It is correct as is.

Revising and Editing Quizzes

Set 2

Instructions

Read each passage. Each passage is followed by questions.

For each multiple-choice question, read the question carefully. Then select the best answer. Fill in the circle for the correct answer.

For other types of questions, follow the instructions given.

Building Your Vocabulary

As you read the passages, list any words you do not understand below. Use a dictionary to look up the meaning of the word. Write the meaning of the word below.

Word: _____

Meaning: _____

_____

Word: _____

Meaning: _____

_____

Word: _____

Meaning: _____

_____

Word: _____

Meaning: _____

_____

Word: _____

Meaning: _____

_____

Quiz 6

Read the passage below. Then answer the questions that follow it.

Paper Planes

Ben sat at the table with Terry, neatly folding pieces of paper. They was making paper planes. Every plane Ben made was perfect. Terry, on the other hand, never seemed to make one that could fly. Terry tried to fly his latest plane across the room. It fell to the ground like it was made of lead. Terry banged his hand on the table.

"I'm not making any more planes! Terry said."

Ben took Terry's plane and adjusted a few folds. It glided threw the air!

"Maybe I'll try just a few more," Terry said.

1   Read this sentence from the passage.

   Ben took Terry's plane and adjusted a few folds.

   Which word means about the same as *adjusted*?
   Ⓐ   removed

   Ⓑ   checked

   Ⓒ   changed

   Ⓓ   made

2 What is the correct way to punctuate the sentence below?

"I'm not making any more planes! Terry said."

Ⓐ "I'm not making any more planes"! Terry said.

Ⓑ "I'm not making any more planes!" Terry said.

Ⓒ "I'm not making any more planes! Terry" said.

Ⓓ "I'm not making any more planes!" Terry said."

3 Which change should be made in the third paragraph?

Ⓐ Change *took* to *taking*

Ⓑ Change *Terry's* to *Terrys*

Ⓒ Change *threw* to *through*

Ⓓ There is no change needed.

4 In paragraph 1, which word would best replace the phrase "on the other hand"?

Ⓐ however

Ⓑ also

Ⓒ nearly

Ⓓ besides

5 Which of these shows the correct way to write sentence 2?

Ⓐ They were making paper planes.

Ⓑ They is making paper planes.

Ⓒ They will be making paper planes.

Ⓓ They are making paper planes.

Quiz 7

Read the passage below. Then answer the questions that follow it.

My School Friends

 It's very important to have friends. They help you when you feel lonely. They are fun to share secrets with too. My best friends are Link Beth and Sally. They all go to my school and are in the same class as I. Sally is my best friend as well as my cousin.

We always make sure to behave good in class so the teacher allows us to sit beside each other. Sometimes we can't help but laugh with each other. It is especially hard when Beth tells us jokes. She is the most funny friend I have. That is when the teacher makes us move apart.

1   Read this sentence from the passage.

We always make sure to behave good in class so the teacher allows us to sit beside each other.

Which word could best replace *good* in the sentence?

Ⓐ   fine

Ⓑ   goodness

Ⓒ   nice

Ⓓ   well

2   Which of these shows the correct punctuation of the sentence below?

My best friends are Link Beth and Sally.

Ⓐ   My best friends, are, Link Beth and Sally.

Ⓑ   My best friends are Link Beth, and Sally.

Ⓒ   My best friends are Link, Beth, and Sally.

Ⓓ   My best friends are, Link, Beth, and Sally.

3   Which word should replace the word *I* in the sentence below?

They all go to my school and are in the same class as I.

Ⓐ   me

Ⓑ   mine

Ⓒ   my

Ⓓ   ours

4   Which word or words should replace the underlined words below?

She is the <u>most funny</u> friend I have.

Ⓐ   funnier

Ⓑ   funniest

Ⓒ   more funny

Ⓓ   more funnier

Quiz 8

Read the passage below. Then answer the questions that follow it.

Dolphins

(1) Dolphins are marine mammals. (2) Many people mistake dolphins as being a type of fish. (3) They look similar to fish. (4) Dolphins are actually mammals. (5) All fish have gills, but dolphins do not.

(6) Dolphins are close relatives of both whales and porpoises. (7) There are over 40 different species of dolphins. (8) They are located worldwide. (9) They live mostly in shallow and tropical waters.

(10) They are very intelligent mammals. (11) They can be trained to do a range of things. (12) They are well known for being able to perform tricks. (13) Dolphin shows entertain people by having dolphins perform these tricks. (14) In these shows, people sometimes even surf on dolphins.

1   Where would be the best place to add the sentence below?

> **You can tell that dolphins are not fish because they lack the features of fish.**

    Ⓐ   Before sentence 1

    Ⓑ   After sentence 4

    Ⓒ   After sentence 6

    Ⓓ   After sentence 9

2 Which transition word could best be added to the start of sentence 9?

Ⓐ Finally,

Ⓑ However,

Ⓒ Meanwhile,

Ⓓ Then,

3 What is the best way to combine sentences 3 and 4?

Ⓐ They look similar to fish, so dolphins are actually mammals.

Ⓑ They look similar to fish, or dolphins are actually mammals.

Ⓒ They look similar to fish, and dolphins are actually mammals.

Ⓓ They look similar to fish, but dolphins are actually mammals.

4 Which sentence is the topic sentence of paragraph 3?

Ⓐ Sentence 10

Ⓑ Sentence 11

Ⓒ Sentence 13

Ⓓ Sentence 14

5 Where would be the best place to add the sentence below?

If you ever get the chance, you should see a dolphin show.

Ⓐ At the end of paragraph 1

Ⓑ At the beginning of paragraph 2

Ⓒ At the end of paragraph 2

Ⓓ At the end of paragraph 3

Quiz 9

Read the passage below. Then answer the questions that follow it.

Davy Crockett

Have you ever heard of Davy Crockett. You might have heard about the amazing things that he did. Davy Crockett was born on August 17th 1786. He was known for being a brave Hunter and also telling tall tales. One tall tale that he told was about being able to shoot a bullet at an ax and split it in halves. Many of his tall tales describe things that were impossibel. It seems silly that people believed the tales, but they did.

Davy Crockett married Mary Finley in 1806. His first son, John, was born in 1807. He had another son, William, in 1809. His only daughter, Margaret, was born in 1812.

Davy Crockett could not read or write until he was eighteen years old! He later became a soldier, and then a politician. He became a member of Congress in 1833. He died at the Alamo in 1836.

1   What is the correct way to write the first sentence?

    Ⓐ   Have you ever heard of Davy Crockett!

    Ⓑ   Have you ever heard of Davy Crockett?

    Ⓒ   Have you ever heard of Davy Crockett,

    Ⓓ   It is correct as it is.

2 Which of these shows the correct way to punctuate the sentence below?

Davy Crockett was born on August 17th 1786.

Ⓐ   Davy Crockett was born on, August 17th 1786.

Ⓑ   Davy Crockett was born on August, 17th 1786.

Ⓒ   Davy Crockett was born on August 17th, 1786.

Ⓓ   Davy Crockett was born on August, 17th, 1786.

3 Which word from the passage should NOT be capitalized?

Ⓐ   August

Ⓑ   Hunter

Ⓒ   Finley

Ⓓ   Alamo

4 What is the correct way to spell *impossibel*?

Ⓐ   impossible

Ⓑ   impossibbel

Ⓒ   impossibble

Ⓓ   impossable

5 Which change should be made in the first paragraph?

Ⓐ   Change *amazing* to *amazzing*

Ⓑ   Change *shoot* to *shot*

Ⓒ   Change *halves* to *half*

Ⓓ   There is no change needed.

Quiz 10

Read the passage below. Then answer the questions that follow it.

What is Your Color?

Today in class, we had a survey of eye color and hair color. I have black hair and green eyes. Fifteen people had brown hair. Five had blond hair. Three had black hair. There was only one person with red hair.

I am the only one in my class with green eyes. There were 15 people with brown eyes. That was more then half of the class. Only eight people had blue eyes. To show the results, on the chalkboard we put a chart up. I think it's great that we live in a world with so many diffrent kinds of people.

1   Read the sentences below.

> **Fifteen people had brown hair. Five had blond hair. Three had black hair.**

What is the correct way to combine the sentences?

Ⓐ   Fifteen people had brown hair, five blond, three black.

Ⓑ   Fifteen people had brown hair, five blond, and three black.

Ⓒ   Fifteen people had brown hair, five had blond hair, and three had black hair.

Ⓓ   Fifteen people had brown, five had blond, and three had black, hair.

2 What is the best way to rewrite the sentence below?

To show the results, on the chalkboard we put a chart up.

Ⓐ We put a chart up to show the results on the chalkboard.

Ⓑ We put on the chalkboard to show the results a chart up.

Ⓒ We put on the chalkboard a chart up to show the results.

Ⓓ We put a chart up on the chalkboard to show the results.

3 Which change should be made in the sentence below?

That was more then half of the class.

Ⓐ Change *was* to *were*

Ⓑ Change *then* to *than*

Ⓒ Change *half* to *halves*

Ⓓ There is no change needed.

4 Which change should be made in the last sentence?

Ⓐ Change *it's* to *its*

Ⓑ Change *diffrent* to *different*

Ⓒ Change *kinds* to *kind*

Ⓓ There is no change needed.

Revising and Editing Quizzes

Set 3

Instructions

Read each passage. Each passage is followed by questions.

For each multiple-choice question, read the question carefully. Then select the best answer. Fill in the circle for the correct answer.

For other types of questions, follow the instructions given.

Building Your Vocabulary

As you read the passages, list any words you do not understand below. Use a dictionary to look up the meaning of the word. Write the meaning of the word below.

Word: _____

Meaning: _____

_____

Word: _____

Meaning: _____

_____

Word: _____

Meaning: _____

_____

Word: _____

Meaning: _____

_____

Word: _____

Meaning: _____

_____

Quiz 11

Read the passage below. Then answer the questions that follow it.

Wishing Well

I am coin in well.
Here I was throwed and here I fell.
A little boy made a wish.
Now all of my neighbors are fish!
A special day is coming around the bend.
On that day, anuther wish will throw me a friend.

1   Explain what the line below means.

A special day is coming around the bend.

_____

_____

_____

_____

_____

2   Which word should replace *throwed* in line 2?

Ⓐ   threw

Ⓑ   thrown

Ⓒ   threwed

Ⓓ   throw

3   Which word in the poem is spelled incorrectly?

Ⓐ   little

Ⓑ   neighbors

Ⓒ   around

Ⓓ   anuther

4   Which line from the poem is NOT a complete sentence?

Ⓐ   I am coin in well.

Ⓑ   A little boy made a wish.

Ⓒ   Now all of my neighbors are fish!

Ⓓ   A special day is coming around the bend.

5   Which change should be made in line 5?

Ⓐ   Change *day* to *Day*

Ⓑ   Change *is* to *are*

Ⓒ   Change *coming* to *comming*

Ⓓ   There is no change needed.

Quiz 12

Read the passage below. Then answer the questions that follow it.

Ducks

Ducks are small aquatic birds that usually live next to water. They can be found by fresh water and they can be found by sea water. They are found all over the world.

A male duck is called a drake. Female ducks are usually just called ducks, but can be called hens. Baby ducks are known as ducklings.

Ducks eat a variety of food including worms, plants, and small insects. Ducks have not any nerves in their feet. This allows them to hunt for there food without being affected by the cold of the water.

1   Which of these is the best way to rewrite the sentence below?

They can be found by fresh water and they can be found by sea water.

Ⓐ   They can be found by fresh water and by sea water.

Ⓑ   They can be found by fresh sea water.

Ⓒ   They can be found by fresh water and found by sea water.

Ⓓ   They can be found by fresh water sea water.

2 Which word would best replace the words "next to" in the first sentence?

Ⓐ   beside

Ⓑ   under

Ⓒ   about

Ⓓ   nearby

3 Which of these is the correct way to rewrite the sentence below?

Ducks have not any nerves in their feet.

Ⓐ   Ducks have no nerves in their feet.

Ⓑ   Ducks have none nerves in their feet.

Ⓒ   Ducks not have any nerves in their feet.

Ⓓ   Ducks have not nerves in their feet.

4 Which word from the passage contains a silent letter?

Ⓐ   small

Ⓑ   fresh

Ⓒ   water

Ⓓ   known

5 Which change should be made in the last sentence?

Ⓐ   Change *allows* to *allow*

Ⓑ   Change *there* to *their*

Ⓒ   Change *without* to *with out*

Ⓓ   No change is needed.

Quiz 13

Read the passage below. Then answer the questions that follow it.

Careless Cooks

Aaron and Judy were making a cake. First they put in the flour and eggs. Next Judy found the cake tin while Aaron finished the cake mix. They poured it into the cake tin, put it in the oven, and went outside to play. They tired themselves out, so Aaron and Judy decided to go for a nap. An afternoon nap can be a good way to recharge.

When they woke up, something smelled odd. They suddenly remembered their cake! It was too late. They went into the kitchen. When they took it out of the oven, the cake was black and crunchy. They knew write away that it would not taste great. They had to throw it out.

1   Read this sentence from the passage.

   They went into the kitchen.

   Which word could best replace *went* to show that Aaron and Judy went to the kitchen quickly?

   Ⓐ   walked

   Ⓑ   strolled

   Ⓒ   raced

   Ⓓ   drove

2 Which of these is the best way to change the last sentence?

Ⓐ Sadly, they had to throw it out.

Ⓑ Strangely, they had to throw it out.

Ⓒ Suddenly, they had to throw it out.

Ⓓ Surely, they had to throw it out.

3 Which sentence does NOT belong in the passage?

Ⓐ *First they put in the flour and eggs.*

Ⓑ *An afternoon nap can be a good way to recharge.*

Ⓒ *When they woke up, something smelled odd.*

Ⓓ *When they took it out of the oven, the cake was black and crunchy.*

4 In the word *recharge*, what does the prefix *re-* mean?

Ⓐ before

Ⓑ toward

Ⓒ again

Ⓓ more

5 Which change should be made in the sentence below?

They knew write away that it would not taste great.

Ⓐ Change *knew* to *new*

Ⓑ Change *write* to *right*

Ⓒ Change *would* to *wood*

Ⓓ Change *great* to *grate*

Quiz 14

Read the passage below. Then answer the questions that follow it.

Day Dreaming

Sometimes I wonder what it would be like to be a bird. I would love to spread my wings and fly far and wide. Would fly all around the world. I would zoom across oceans to find new places.

First I would see the Pyramids in Egypt. Then I would drift over to England on a soft breze to visit the Queen. I would perch on top of the Eiffel Tower in Paris. I would like seeing the view. Then I would pick my next place to visit. But for now, I just have to finish my Homework.

1   Place the following words from the passage in alphabetical order.

across   around   all

_____   _____   _____

places   perch   pick

_____   _____   _____

fly   first   find   finish

_____   _____   _____   _____

wonder   would   wings   wide

_____   _____   _____   _____

2 Which word in the last paragraph does NOT need to start with a capital?

Ⓐ   Egypt

Ⓑ   Eiffel

Ⓒ   Paris

Ⓓ   Homework

3 Which sentence from paragraph 1 is NOT a complete sentence?

Ⓐ   *Sometimes I wonder what it would be like to be a bird.*

Ⓑ   *I would love to spread my wings and fly far and wide.*

Ⓒ   *Would fly all around the world.*

Ⓓ   *I would zoom across oceans to find new places.*

4 How should the word *breze* be spelled?

Ⓐ   breeze

Ⓑ   brieze

Ⓒ   breize

Ⓓ   breez

5 Which of these is the best way to rewrite the sentence below?

I would like seeing the view.

Ⓐ   I would see the view.

Ⓑ   I would enjoy the view.

Ⓒ   I would take the view.

Ⓓ   I would understand the view.

Quiz 15

Read the passage below. Then answer the questions that follow it.

Glass

Glass is an everyday material found everywhere from bottles to windows. It is also recyclable. This means that it can be reused! It is important to recycle glass because it means less new glass needs to be made. This saves a lot of chemicals from polluting the air. In fact, every metric ton of recycled glass saves 690 pounds of carbon dioxide from polluting the air! Recycling glass also means that there is less waste. There is no need for landfills to be full of glass materials. These materials can and should be recycled!

Each state that is part of America has its own system for recycling glass. Ask an adult in your state how you can help with recycling glass. Then make the effort to change your ways. You'll be glad you did and the Earth will too!

1   The word *recyclable* is made by adding the suffix *-able* to the base word *recycle*. The word *recyclable* means "able to be recycled." Notice that the *e* is dropped from the end of *recycle* when the suffix is added. Add a suffix to the base words below to make a word with the given meaning.

Base Word	Meaning	New Word
wash	able to be washed	
break	able to be broken	
believe	able to be believed	
enjoy	able to be enjoyed	

2   What is the best way to rewrite the sentence below?

Each state that is part of America has its own system for recycling glass.

Ⓐ   Each state America has its own system for recycling glass.

Ⓑ   Each America's states has its own system for recycling glass.

Ⓒ   Each American state has its own system for recycling glass.

Ⓓ   Each America state has its own system for recycling glass.

3   Which word could replace *everyday* in the first sentence without changing the meaning of the sentence?

Ⓐ   nice

Ⓑ   special

Ⓒ   common

Ⓓ   useful

4   In the last sentence, what is the word *you'll* short for?

Ⓐ   You all

Ⓑ   You will

Ⓒ   You could

Ⓓ   You should

5   Which sentence should NOT end with an exclamation mark?

Ⓐ   This means that it can be reused!

Ⓑ   In fact, every metric ton of recycled glass saves 690 pounds of carbon dioxide from polluting the air!

Ⓒ   These materials can and should be recycled!

Ⓓ   You'll be glad you did and the Earth will too!

Revising and Editing Quizzes

Set 4

Instructions

Read each passage. Each passage is followed by questions.

For each multiple-choice question, read the question carefully. Then select the best answer. Fill in the circle for the correct answer.

For other types of questions, follow the instructions given.

Building Your Vocabulary

As you read the passages, list any words you do not understand below. Use a dictionary to look up the meaning of the word. Write the meaning of the word below.

Word: _____

Meaning: _____

_____

Word: _____

Meaning: _____

_____

Word: _____

Meaning: _____

_____

Word: _____

Meaning: _____

_____

Word: _____

Meaning: _____

_____

Quiz 16

Read the passage below. Then answer the questions that follow it.

Bananas

A banana is a type of fruit that grows on a tree. Bananas will grow in bunches on the tree. They can be eaten as a snack or in meals or desserts. Wild bananas may contain seeds. However, the bananas grown on banana farms have been grown in such a way that they will not. When bananas are picked, they are green. While they are shipped all over the world, they ripen and turn yellow.

When buying bananas in a store, you should buy bright yellow ones if you are going to eat them right away. You should buy ones that are slightly green if you are going to eat them in a few days. Bananas that have started to turn black will be soft and mushy. You should only use these to bake things like banana bread or banana muffins.

1   The word *picked* is the base word *pick* with the suffix *-ed* added. The word *shipped* is the base word *ship* with the suffix *-ed* added. When the suffix is added, the *p* is doubled. For each word below, write the word with the suffix *-ed* added to it. Be sure to spell each word correctly.

laugh   _____   pat   _____

waste   _____   rob   _____

clap   _____   hope   _____

talk   _____   pass   _____

joke   _____   drag   _____

2 Which meaning of the word *bright* is used in the sentence below?

> **When buying bananas in a store, you should buy bright yellow ones if you are going to eat them right away.**

Ⓐ strong in color

Ⓑ smart

Ⓒ happy or cheerful

Ⓓ likely to be successful

3 Which word should replace the word *eated* in the sentence below?

> **They can be eated as a snack or in meals or desserts.**

Ⓐ eat

Ⓑ eating

Ⓒ eats

Ⓓ eaten

4 Which word from the passage is an adjective?

Ⓐ tree

Ⓑ bunches

Ⓒ ripen

Ⓓ yellow

5 Which of these is the past tense form of *buy*?

Ⓐ buys

Ⓑ buyed

Ⓒ bought

Ⓓ boughted

Quiz 17

Read the passage below. Then answer the questions that follow it.

The Desert Life

 The cowboy wandered, through the desert. He and his horse betty had been partners for four years. He liked the feeling of the sand in his boots. The smell of fresh cactus hung in the air. He didn't think he would have it any other way.

He lay down in the warm dirt. His hat was resting on his chest. He watched the sun set to the west. The sky glowed orange, and then faded to pink.

Life doesn't get much better than this, he said.

1   The author says that the smell of cactus "hung in the air." What does the phrase "hung in the air" mean?

_____

_____

_____

_____

_____

_____

2 What change should be made in the first sentence?

Ⓐ Delete the comma

Ⓑ Replace *through* with *threw*

Ⓒ Change *cowboy* to *cow boy*

Ⓓ No change is needed.

3 What is the correct way to combine the sentences below?

He lay down in the warm dirt. His hat was resting on his chest.

Ⓐ He lay down in the warm dirt and his hat resting on his chest.

Ⓑ He lay down in the warm dirt so his hat resting on his chest.

Ⓒ He lay down in the warm dirt with his hat resting on his chest.

Ⓓ He lay down in the warm dirt while his hat resting on his chest.

4 What is the correct way to punctuate the last sentence?

Ⓐ "Life doesn't get much better than this" he said.

Ⓑ "Life doesn't get much better than this," he said.

Ⓒ "Life doesn't get much better than this, he said."

Ⓓ "Life doesn't get much better than this," he said."

5 Which word in the passage should start with a capital letter?

Ⓐ betty

Ⓑ cactus

Ⓒ west

Ⓓ sky

Quiz 18

Read the passage below. Then answer the questions that follow it.

One Dollar Bill

(1) The most commonest form of currency in the United States is the one dollar bill. (2) It was designed by Gilbert Stuart. (3) It features a picture of George Washington on one side. (4) The picture of George Washington was also painted by Gilbert Stuart. (5) The other side of the one dollar bill shows the Great Seal of the United States.

(6) The dollar bill was first issued in 1862. (7) It looked much different than it does today. (8) The dollar bill you see today wasn't introduced until 1969.

The front and back of today's dollar bill is shown on the left. The front of the first dollar bill is shown above.

1   The words *front* and *back* are antonyms, or words with opposite meanings. For each word below, write a word with the opposite meaning.

dark   _____   begin _____

easy   _____   neat _____

cheap   _____   deep _____

quiet   _____   dry _____

2   Which words should replace the term "most commonest" in sentence 1?

  Ⓐ   most common

  Ⓑ   more common

  Ⓒ   most commoner

  Ⓓ   more commoner

3   Which transition word would be best to add to the start of sentence 7?

  Ⓐ   However,

  Ⓑ   Nearly,

  Ⓒ   Likewise,

  Ⓓ   Usually,

4   Which sentence would be best to add to the beginning of the passage to state the central idea?

  Ⓐ   Another term for a bill is a note.

  Ⓑ   Most countries have a one dollar bill.

  Ⓒ   There are more coins in America than bills.

  Ⓓ   One dollar bills have a long and interesting history.

5   Where would be the best place to add the sentence below?

  The first dollar bill included a picture of Salmon P. Chase.

  Ⓐ   After sentence 2

  Ⓑ   After sentence 5

  Ⓒ   After sentence 7

  Ⓓ   After sentence 8

Quiz 19

Read the passage below. Then answer the questions that follow it.

The Forest

The sun was setting in the sky. The bright moon were rising above the trees. For a few moments, the forest was still. Then came the crunching of dry leaves as all of the animals came out of hiding. The sound of twigs cracking filled the air.

The animals runned and danced in the cool night air. Fireflies circled above them, their lights twinkling like falling stars. The cold air was a relief after the humid day. The animals shouted and rejoiced at the beautiful night. The buzzing and chirping sounded like a lovely song.

©Oliver Herold

1.   Adjectives are describing words. Complete the table by listing adjectives from the passage and what each adjective is describing.

Adjective	What the Adjective is Describing
bright	the moon

2   Which word should replace the word *runned* in the sentence below?

The animals runned and danced in the cool night air.

Ⓐ   run

Ⓑ   ran

Ⓒ   running

Ⓓ   runner

3   Which change should be made in the second sentence?

Ⓐ   Change *bright* to *brite*

Ⓑ   Change *were* to *was*

Ⓒ   Change *rising* to *riseing*

Ⓓ   There is no change needed.

4   Which transition word or phrase could replace "For a few moments" in the third sentence without changing the meaning of the sentence?

Ⓐ   For example

Ⓑ   At last

Ⓒ   Suddenly

Ⓓ   For a short time

5   What is the base word of the word *beautiful*?

Ⓐ   beaut

Ⓑ   beauty

Ⓒ   ful

Ⓓ   full

Quiz 20

Read the passage below. Then answer the questions that follow it.

Neptune

Neptune is one of the most interesting planets. It has been studied for a long time. However, scientists still do not know everything about it. Neptune was discovered in 1846 by two German astronomers named Heinrich D'Arrest and Johann Galle. There are four gas planets in our Solar System. They are Jupiter, Saturn, Neptune, and Uranus. These planets are larger than all the other planets. Neptune is the smallest gas planet. It still has a radius about 17 times greater than Earth's radius.

In August 1989, the Voyager spacecraft visited Neptune. It is the only time Neptune has been visited. It was found that like Earth the sky on Neptune has clouds in it. There are even some storms on Neptune. In fact, there are large dark spots on Neptune's surface. These dark spots are actually storms, and they usually last for several Years.

1   The word *larger* is used in the first paragraph to compare the gas planets to the other planets. Complete the sentences below to give two more examples of words that are used in the passage to compare things.

The word _____ is used to compare _____

_____.

The word _____ is used to compare _____

_____.

2   What is the correct way to use commas in the sentence below?

It was found that like Earth the sky on Neptune has clouds in it.

Ⓐ   It was found that, like, Earth the sky on Neptune has clouds in it.

Ⓑ   It was found that, like Earth the sky, on Neptune has clouds in it.

Ⓒ   It was found that, like Earth, the sky on Neptune has clouds in it.

Ⓓ   It was found that like Earth, the sky on Neptune, has clouds in it.

3   Which change should be made in the third sentence?

Ⓐ   Delete the comma

Ⓑ   Change *scientists* to *scientist's*

Ⓒ   Change *do* to *does*

Ⓓ   Make no change

4   What is the correct way to spell *studyed*?

Ⓐ   studied

Ⓑ   studdied

Ⓒ   studdyed

Ⓓ   It is correct as it is.

5   Which word in the passage does NOT need to start with a capital letter?

Ⓐ   German

Ⓑ   August

Ⓒ   Voyager

Ⓓ   Years

Section 2
Language, Vocabulary, and Grammar
Quizzes

Instructions

For each multiple-choice question, read the question carefully. Then select the best answer. Fill in the circle for the correct answer.

For other types of questions, follow the instructions given.

Quiz 21: Analyze Words

1   The word *rear* ends in *ear*. Which letter can be added to *ear* to form another word?

(A)   n

(B)   z

(C)   c

(D)   j

2   In which word does *-ear* sound the same as in *bear*?

(A)   wear

(B)   fear

(C)   gear

(D)   hear

3   Which word rhymes with *kiss*?

(A)   miss

(B)   bless

(C)   chess

(D)   kind

4   Which word does NOT rhyme with the three other words?

(A)   oil

(B)   boil

(C)   soil

(D)   fail

Quiz 22: Place Words in Alphabetical Order

1 Which word would go first in alphabetical order?

Ⓐ   form

Ⓑ   forty

Ⓒ   fortune

Ⓓ   four

2 Which word would go first in alphabetical order?

Ⓐ   string

Ⓑ   start

Ⓒ   strong

Ⓓ   sting

3 Which set of words are in alphabetical order?

Ⓐ   hope, hole, hose

Ⓑ   hole, hope, hose

Ⓒ   hose, hole, hope

Ⓓ   hole, hose, hope

4 Using alphabetical order, which word could go between the words?

train, _____, trod

Ⓐ   trust

Ⓑ   treat

Ⓒ   truth

Ⓓ   tame

Quiz 23: Divide Words into Syllables

For each word below, divide the word into two syllables. The first one has been completed for you.

1	carpet	car / pet
2	hopeful	_____
3	letter	_____
4	notice	_____
5	summer	_____
6	happen	_____
7	farmer	_____
8	away	_____

For each word below, divide the word into three syllables. The first one has been completed for you.

9	animal	an / i / mal
10	important	_____
11	basketball	_____
12	butterfly	_____
13	excitement	_____
14	passenger	_____

Quiz 24: Identify and Use Antonyms

1   Which word means the opposite of *full*?

Ⓐ   high

Ⓑ   low

Ⓒ   empty

Ⓓ   fill

2   Which two words have opposite meanings?

Ⓐ   open, closed

Ⓑ   high, height

Ⓒ   cold, windy

Ⓓ   hot, heat

3   Which word means the opposite of *pretty*?

Ⓐ   handsome

Ⓑ   ugly

Ⓒ   noble

Ⓓ   royal

4   Which two words have opposite meanings?

Ⓐ   float, sink

Ⓑ   hard, tough

Ⓒ   walking, jogging

Ⓓ   high, fall

Quiz 25: Identify Base Words

1   What is the base word of *bringing*?

    Ⓐ   brin

    Ⓑ   bring

    Ⓒ   ing

    Ⓓ   ring

2   What is the base word of *teacher*?

    Ⓐ   tea

    Ⓑ   er

    Ⓒ   her

    Ⓓ   teach

3   What is the base word of *rapidly*?

    Ⓐ   rap

    Ⓑ   rapid

    Ⓒ   ly

    Ⓓ   pidly

4   What is the base word of *usually*?

    Ⓐ   all

    Ⓑ   us

    Ⓒ   ly

    Ⓓ   usual

Quiz 26: Use Irregular Plurals

For each question below, select the word that correctly completes the sentence.

1   The two _____ ran out of the room.

    Ⓐ   mouse

    Ⓑ   mice

    Ⓒ   mouses

    Ⓓ   mices

2   Hundreds of _____ ran into the store.

    Ⓐ   woman

    Ⓑ   women

    Ⓒ   womans

    Ⓓ   womens

3   All of the store's _____ were bare.

    Ⓐ   shelfs

    Ⓑ   shelves

    Ⓒ   shelf

    Ⓓ   shelve

4   I have to get all my _____ checked every year.

    Ⓐ   tooth

    Ⓑ   tooths

    Ⓒ   teeths

    Ⓓ   teeth

Quiz 27: Use Words with Suffixes

For each question below, select the word that correctly completes the sentence.

1   It was a cold and _____ day.

    (A)   rain

    (B)   rainy

    (C)   rained

    (D)   raining

2   Michael _____ explained that he was lost and needed help.

    (A)   calmly

    (B)   calmness

    (C)   calming

    (D)   calmer

3   The trick that Morgan played was very _____.

    (A)   childhood

    (B)   children

    (C)   childish

    (D)   childless

4   We had an _____ day at the zoo.

    (A)   enjoyment

    (B)   enjoying

    (C)   enjoyable

    (D)   enjoyed

Quiz 28: Spell Commonly Misspelled Words

For each question below, circle the word in the sentence that is spelled incorrectly. Write the correct spelling of the word on the line.

1   My muther drove me to the mall this morning.

_____

2   My huose is right at the end of the street.

_____

3   I usually catch the bus to scool.

_____

4   I wanted to make my cousin feel wellcome.

_____

5   Jane looked pritty in her new bright yellow dress.

_____

6   I could not deside what to wear to the birthday party.

_____

Quiz 29: Understand and Use Prefixes

1   What does the word *prepack* mean?

Ⓐ   not pack

Ⓑ   pack before

Ⓒ   pack again

Ⓓ   pack after

2   Which prefix can be added to the word *cook* to make a word meaning "cook again"?

Ⓐ   un-

Ⓑ   re-

Ⓒ   mis-

Ⓓ   pre-

3   Which prefix should be added to the word to make the sentence correct?

Greg found his shoe in a very __likely place.

Ⓐ   un-

Ⓑ   re-

Ⓒ   in-

Ⓓ   mis-

4   Which word contains the prefix *pre-*?

Ⓐ   pressed

Ⓑ   prewash

Ⓒ   prefer

Ⓓ   pretty

Quiz 30: Understand and Use Suffixes

1 What does the word *happier* mean?

 Ⓐ in a way that is happy

 Ⓑ the most happy

 Ⓒ someone who is happy

 Ⓓ more happy

2 Which suffix can be added to the word *paint* to make a word meaning "one who paints"?

 Ⓐ -ed

 Ⓑ -ing

 Ⓒ -s

 Ⓓ -er

3 Which word makes the sentence correct?

  John is the _____ person I have ever met.

 Ⓐ kindly

 Ⓑ kinder

 Ⓒ kindest

 Ⓓ kindness

4 Which word means "in a nice way"?

 Ⓐ nicer

 Ⓑ nicest

 Ⓒ nicely

 Ⓓ niceness

Quiz 31: Understand Greek and Latin Word Parts

1   The word *thermos* contains a Greek root meaning –

    Ⓐ   heat

    Ⓑ   tall

    Ⓒ   three

    Ⓓ   new

2   The word *geology* contains the Greek root *geo-*. *Geology* is probably the study of –

    Ⓐ   life

    Ⓑ   water

    Ⓒ   earth

    Ⓓ   people

3   A *monolith* is a type of mountain. What is the meaning of the Greek root *mono-* used in the word *monolith*?

    Ⓐ   one

    Ⓑ   long

    Ⓒ   many

    Ⓓ   heavy

4   The word *decagon* contains the Greek root *deca-*. How many sides does a *decagon* most likely have?

    Ⓐ   5

    Ⓑ   8

    Ⓒ   10

    Ⓓ   12

Quiz 32: Spell Words with Suffixes Correctly

1   Which word is spelled incorrectly?

Ⓐ   creepping

Ⓑ   sniffing

Ⓒ   smelling

Ⓓ   copying

2   Which underlined word is spelled incorrectly?

Ⓐ   <u>scary</u> storm

Ⓑ   <u>lonely</u> rider

Ⓒ   <u>sipping</u> a drink

Ⓓ   <u>visitting</u> a friend

3   Which word is spelled incorrectly?

Ⓐ   laughing

Ⓑ   screamming

Ⓒ   hopeful

Ⓓ   slapping

4   Which underlined word is spelled incorrectly?

Ⓐ   <u>written</u> words

Ⓑ   <u>beautifull</u> garden

Ⓒ   <u>exactly</u> right

Ⓓ   <u>flightless</u> bird

Quiz 33: Use Contractions

A contraction is a shortened form of two words. For example, *I am* can be shortened to *I'm*. For each question below, write the contraction for the two words given. Then write a sentence that uses the contraction.

1   she is   _____

_____

2   we will   _____

_____

3   they are   _____

_____

4   I have   _____

_____

5   he would   _____

_____

6   could not   _____

_____

Quiz 34: Identify and Use Synonyms

1   Which word means about the same as *stir*?

Ⓐ   bowl

Ⓑ   mix

Ⓒ   steer

Ⓓ   shake

2   Which two words have about the same meaning?

Ⓐ   rush, hurry

Ⓑ   yawn, tired

Ⓒ   plain, plane

Ⓓ   cheerful, sad

3   Which word means about the same as *pleasant*?

Ⓐ   annoying

Ⓑ   playful

Ⓒ   curious

Ⓓ   nice

4   Which two words have about the same meaning?

Ⓐ   scream, yell

Ⓑ   steep, deep

Ⓒ   fast, slow

Ⓓ   sunny, day

Quiz 35: Identify Types of Words

1   Which word in the sentence is a verb?

The bell in the tower rang ten times.

Ⓐ   bell

Ⓑ   tower

Ⓒ   rang

Ⓓ   times

2   Which word in the sentence is an adjective?

I looked out the window and saw a beautiful rainbow.

Ⓐ   looked

Ⓑ   window

Ⓒ   beautiful

Ⓓ   rainbow

3   Which word in the sentence is a noun?

The pool was colder than it had ever been.

Ⓐ   pool

Ⓑ   colder

Ⓒ   ever

Ⓓ   been

Quiz 36: Use Verbs Correctly

1   Which word makes the sentence correct?

I decided to _____ the water on the stove.

Ⓐ   boiled

Ⓑ   boiling

Ⓒ   boils

Ⓓ   boil

2   Which word or words make the sentence correct?

Sam _____ me lightly on the arm.

Ⓐ   punch

Ⓑ   punched

Ⓒ   is punched

Ⓓ   punching

3   Which sentence is written correctly?

Ⓐ   I will have to rush to be home on time.

Ⓑ   I will have to rushes to be home on time.

Ⓒ   I will have to rushed to be home on time.

Ⓓ   I will have to rushing to be home on time.

Quiz 37: Use Correct Verb Tense

For each question below, choose the correct verb tense to complete the sentence.

1   The teacher _____ cross if we are late to class.

    Ⓐ   am

    Ⓑ   was

    Ⓒ   will be

    Ⓓ   have been

2   We _____ down two wrong streets before finding the store.

    Ⓐ   drive

    Ⓑ   drove

    Ⓒ   have driven

    Ⓓ   had driven

3   Next week, I _____ to the class about recycling.

    Ⓐ   speak

    Ⓑ   spoke

    Ⓒ   will speak

    Ⓓ   have spoken

4   I usually _____ baseball every weekend.

    Ⓐ   play

    Ⓑ   have played

    Ⓒ   played

    Ⓓ   did play

Quiz 38: Use Pronouns

For each question below, choose the pronoun that best completes the sentence.

1   Chloe put _____ bag down.

    Ⓐ   him

    Ⓑ   its

    Ⓒ   her

    Ⓓ   she

2   Brian made _____ a sandwich.

    Ⓐ   himself

    Ⓑ   itself

    Ⓒ   themselves

    Ⓓ   yourselves

3   Anna watched a movie. She said _____ was good.

    Ⓐ   us

    Ⓑ   it

    Ⓒ   them

    Ⓓ   her

4   I asked Tim to wait for _____ after school.

    Ⓐ   I

    Ⓑ   my

    Ⓒ   mine

    Ⓓ   me

Quiz 39: Use Possessive Pronouns

For each question below, choose the pronoun that best completes the sentence.

1   Tyra owns the bike. It is _____.

    Ⓐ   mine

    Ⓑ   hers

    Ⓒ   yours

    Ⓓ   theirs

2   Mike and Ryan live in that house. It is _____ house.

    Ⓐ   they

    Ⓑ   them

    Ⓒ   their

    Ⓓ   his

3   I like drawing. Drawing is _____ hobby.

    Ⓐ   my

    Ⓑ   me

    Ⓒ   mine

    Ⓓ   I

4   "I see you have a new haircut. I think _____ hair looks good."

    Ⓐ   you

    Ⓑ   your

    Ⓒ   her

    Ⓓ   its

Quiz 40: Understand Word Meanings

1   What does the word *amusing* mean in the sentence below?

Shelley laughed a lot because the book was very amusing.

Ⓐ   reading

Ⓑ   funny

Ⓒ   important

Ⓓ   giggling

2   What does the word *boring* mean in the sentence below?

Jacob thinks that cleaning his room is a boring task.

Ⓐ   exciting

Ⓑ   dull

Ⓒ   needed

Ⓓ   tidy

3   What does the word *quickly* mean in the sentence below?

The fan blades spun quickly.

Ⓐ   slow

Ⓑ   noisy

Ⓒ   fast

Ⓓ   high

Quiz 41: Spell Words Correctly

1 Which underlined word is spelled incorrectly?

Ⓐ silent night

Ⓑ tall tower

Ⓒ to feel tyred

Ⓓ message in a bottle

2 Which underlined word is spelled incorrectly?

Ⓐ dark tunnel

Ⓑ turkey sandwech

Ⓒ smooth table

Ⓓ fast pitcher

3 Which underlined word is spelled incorrectly?

Ⓐ cellar door

Ⓑ dimond ring

Ⓒ famous people

Ⓓ butcher shop

4 Which underlined word is spelled incorrectly?

Ⓐ hot desert

Ⓑ good reason

Ⓒ red buckett

Ⓓ sunny beach

Quiz 42: Use Correct Punctuation

1   Which sentence has correct punctuation?

Ⓐ   Ray is running late,

Ⓑ   The room is very messy?

Ⓒ   Do you know what time it is?

Ⓓ   Why is Tara sitting by herself.

2   Which sentence has correct punctuation?

Ⓐ   The Japanese flag is red, and, white.

Ⓑ   The wallpaper was yellow, green, and red.

Ⓒ   Arnold has a dog a cat, and two birds.

Ⓓ   I went shopping with Amy Jackie and Rita.

3   Which underlined word is written correctly?

Ⓐ   Theyre running late.

Ⓑ   I'd like to have a day off.

Ⓒ   It was'nt my bike.

Ⓓ   Its getting late now.

4   Choose the answer that shows the correct punctuation.

Ⓐ   "What is the time," Joy asked.

Ⓑ   "Are you busy?" Donnie asked."

Ⓒ   "Wait for me!" Megan yelled."

Ⓓ   "Let's go home," said Chan.

Quiz 43: Use Correct Capitalization

1   Choose the answer that shows the correct capitalization.

   Ⓐ   I am going to a party on Friday Night.

   Ⓑ   The parade passed down John street.

   Ⓒ   Aunt rita often wears colorful dresses.

   Ⓓ   Darren moved here from Miami, Florida.

2   Choose the answer that shows the correct capitalization.

   Ⓐ   Miss dawson is a math teacher.

   Ⓑ   My favorite band is called Sixteen Sounds.

   Ⓒ   I have a pen friend from canada.

   Ⓓ   Jackson said that mexico is hot in summer.

3   Choose the answer that shows the correct capitalization.

   Ⓐ   Donna was born in april.

   Ⓑ   I would like to visit france one day.

   Ⓒ   Our School held a fun run.

   Ⓓ   The nearest bus stop is on George Street.

4   Choose the answer that shows the correct capitalization.

   Ⓐ   Anna wants to be a Dentist one day.

   Ⓑ   My cat's name is ginger.

   Ⓒ   It rains a lot in seattle.

   Ⓓ   My mother often works late on Monday.

Quiz 44: Identify Base Words and Suffixes

For each question below, write the base word and the suffix on the lines.

1   saving

    Base word: _____   Suffix: _____

2   waited

    Base word: _____   Suffix: _____

3   slapped

    Base word: _____   Suffix: _____

4   freezing

    Base word: _____   Suffix: _____

5   glides

    Base word: _____   Suffix: _____

6   listener

    Base word: _____   Suffix: _____

Quiz 45: Use Homonyms and Homophones

1 Which sentence is written correctly?

Ⓐ   I am going to reed a tail.

Ⓑ   I am going to read a tale.

Ⓒ   I am going to reed a tale.

Ⓓ   I am going to read a tail.

2 In which sentence does *mine* mean the same as below?

My Dad works at the local mine.

Ⓐ   That ball is mine.

Ⓑ   My grandfather has an old war mine.

Ⓒ   We visited a gold mine.

Ⓓ   That cake is mine and I'm going to eat it.

3 Which word can be used to complete both sentences?

Tony could not find a tie to _____ his shirt.
Morgan used a _____ to light the candle.

Ⓐ   suit

Ⓑ   match

Ⓒ   flame

Ⓓ   fire

Quiz 46: Use Homographs

Homographs are words that are spelled the same, but have different meanings. For example, the word *bill* can mean "a piece of paper money" or can mean "a beak." For each word below, write two different meanings of the word.

1 bark 1. _____

 2. _____

2 well 1. _____

 2. _____

3 blue 1. _____

 2. _____

4 light 1. _____

 2. _____

5 yard 1. _____

 2. _____

Quiz 47: Write Complete Sentences

Choose the word or words that correctly completes each sentence below.

1   The dog chased Andrew down the _____.

Ⓐ   street

Ⓑ   fast

Ⓒ   all the way

Ⓓ   felt scared

2   The _____ looked bright and beautiful.

Ⓐ   rainbow

Ⓑ   colorful

Ⓒ   in the sky

Ⓓ   after the rain

3   The camera takes good photos and is easy _____.

Ⓐ   to use

Ⓑ   learning

Ⓒ   snapshots

Ⓓ   carry around

4   The roaring fire kept us warm on the _____ night.

Ⓐ   shiver

Ⓑ   very chilly

Ⓒ   burning bright

Ⓓ   lots of firewood

Quiz 48: Use Coordinating Conjunctions

1   Which sentence best combines the two sentences?

I entered a song contest.
I didn't win.

Ⓐ   I entered a song contest, I didn't win.

Ⓑ   I entered a song contest, but I didn't win.

Ⓒ   I entered a song contest, so I didn't win.

Ⓓ   I entered a song contest, then I didn't win.

2   Which sentence best combines the two sentences?

Joanna left the cake in the oven too long.
The cake burned.

Ⓐ   Joanna left the cake in the oven too long, but it burned.

Ⓑ   Joanna left the cake in the oven too long, then it burned.

Ⓒ   Joanna left the cake in the oven too long, so it burned.

Ⓓ   Joanna left the cake in the oven too long, it burned.

3   Which word best completes the sentence below?

They said we had little chance of winning, _____ we remained hopeful.

Ⓐ   for

Ⓑ   and

Ⓒ   nor

Ⓓ   yet

Answer Key

The state standards for Texas are known as the Texas Essential Knowledge and Skills, or TEKS. These standards describe what students are expected to know. Student learning is based on these standards throughout the year, and the state test includes questions that assess whether students have the skills described in the standards.

Each question in Section 1 of this book assesses one skill described in the TEKS. The answer key identifies the skill covered by each question.

Section 1: Revising and Editing Quizzes

Set 1

Quiz 1

Question	Answer	Revising and Editing Skill
1	C	Revise sentences for clarity and coherence
2	D	Use pronouns correctly
3	C	Use irregular verbs correctly
4	B	Use homophones correctly*
5	A	Understand the meaning of idioms

*Homophones are words that are pronounced the same but have different meanings, such as the words *ate* and *eight*.

Quiz 2

Question	Answer	Revising and Editing Skill
1	See Below	Place words in alphabetical order
2	B	Use correct capitalization
3	B	Use words with suffixes correctly
4	C	Spell words correctly
5	C	Use contractions correctly

Q1. The student should list the words in the order below:

- seals, shore, survive
- bears, because, burgers
- large, like, live

Quiz 3

Question	Answer	Revising and Editing Skill
1	See Below	Identify different types of words
2	B	Use correct capitalization
3	A	Spell words correctly
4	C	Revise sentences for clarity and coherence
5	C	Revise passages for clarity and relevance

Q1.   The student should list any three of the verbs and nouns below:
- Verbs: feed, found, move, spread, pollinates
- Nouns: bees, nectar, pollen, flowers, process

Quiz 4

Question	Answer	Revising and Editing Skill
1	See Below	Identify compound words
2	A	Identify different types of words
3	C	Choose a relevant topic sentence
4	A	Use correct verbs and correct verb tense
5	C	Use homophones correctly*

*Homophones are words that are pronounced the same but have different meanings, such as the words *ate* and *eight*.

Q1.   The student should circle the compound words listed below:
- saucepan, teaspoon, hotplate

Quiz 5

Question	Answer	Revising and Editing Skill
1	See Below	Use contractions correctly
2	C	Identify rhyming words
3	B	Use irregular verbs correctly
4	D	Use coordinating conjunctions correctly
5	B	Use correct punctuation (dates)

Q1.   The student should write the following long form of each contraction:
- did not, It is, I am, can not

Set 2

Quiz 6

Question	Answer	Revising and Editing Skill
1	C	Identify and use synonyms
2	B	Use correct punctuation (dialogue)
3	C	Use homophones correctly*
4	A	Understand and use transition words and phrases
5	A	Use correct verbs and correct verb tense

*Homophones are words that are pronounced the same but have different meanings, such as the words *ate* and *eight*.

Quiz 7

Question	Answer	Revising and Editing Skill
1	D	Revise sentences for clarity and correctness
2	C	Use correct punctuation (commas in a series)
3	A	Use pronouns correctly
4	B	Use superlative adjectives correctly*

*Superlative adjectives are formed by adding the suffix *-est* to a word.

Quiz 8

Question	Answer	Revising and Editing Skill
1	B	Revise passages for organization
2	B	Understand and use transition words and phrases
3	D	Combine sentences correctly
4	A	Identify a topic sentence
5	D	Revise passages for organization

Quiz 9

Question	Answer	Revising and Editing Skill
1	B	Use correct punctuation (end punctuation)
2	C	Use correct punctuation (dates)
3	B	Use correct capitalization
4	A	Spell words correctly
5	C	Use singular and plural forms correctly

Quiz 10

Question	Answer	Revising and Editing Skill
1	C	Combine sentences correctly
2	D	Revise sentences for clarity and coherence
3	B	Use words correctly (commonly confused words)
4	B	Spell words correctly

Set 3

Quiz 11

Question	Answer	Revising and Editing Skill
1	See Below	Understand the meaning of idioms
2	B	Use correct verbs and correct verb tense
3	D	Spell words correctly
4	A	Identify complete and incomplete sentences
5	D	Edit sentences for correctness

Q1. The student should explain that the line means that the day is coming soon. The student should show an understanding that the phrase "around the bend" is not meant literally.

Quiz 12

Question	Answer	Revising and Editing Skill
1	A	Revise sentences for clarity and coherence
2	A	Use prepositions correctly
3	A	Edit sentences for correctness
4	D	Identify words with silent letters
5	B	Use homophones correctly*

*Homophones are words that are pronounced the same but have different meanings, such as the words *ate* and *eight*.

Quiz 13

Question	Answer	Revising and Editing Skill
1	C	Choose words to convey meaning
2	A	Understand and use transition words and phrases
3	B	Revise passages for clarity and relevance
4	C	Understand the meaning of prefixes
5	B	Use homophones correctly*

*Homophones are words that are pronounced the same but have different meanings, such as the words *ate* and *eight*.

Quiz 14

Question	Answer	Revising and Editing Skill
1	See Below	Place words in alphabetical order
2	D	Use correct capitalization
3	C	Identify complete and incomplete sentences
4	A	Spell words correctly
5	B	Revise sentences for clarity and correctness

Q1. The student should list the words in the order below:
- across, all, around
- perch, pick, places
- find, finish, first, fly
- wide, wings, wonder, would

Quiz 15

Question	Answer	Revising and Editing Skill
1	See Below	Forms words by adding suffixes
2	C	Revise sentences for clarity and coherence
3	C	Identify and use synonyms
4	B	Use contractions correctly
5	A	Use correct punctuation (end punctuation)

Q1. The student should complete the table with the words below, and each word should be spelled correctly:
- washable, breakable, believable, enjoyable

Set 4

Quiz 16

Question	Answer	Revising and Editing Skill
1	See Below	Form words by adding suffixes
2	A	Determine the meaning of words with multiple meanings
3	D	Use correct verbs and correct verb tense
4	D	Identify different types of words
5	C	Use irregular verbs correctly

Q1. The student should list the words below, and each word should be spelled correctly:
- laughed, wasted, clapped, talked, joked, patted, robbed, hoped, passed, dragged

Quiz 17

Question	Answer	Revising and Editing Skill
1	See Below	Understand the meaning of idioms
2	A	Edit sentences for correctness
3	C	Combine sentences correctly
4	B	Use correct punctuation (dialogue)
5	A	Use correct capitalization

Q1. The student should explain that the phrase "hung in the air" means that the smell stayed in the air, or could be smelled in the air. The student should show an understanding that the phrase "hung in the air" is not meant literally.

Quiz 18

Question	Answer	Revising and Editing Skill
1	See Below	Identify and use antonyms
2	A	Use superlative phrases correctly*
3	A	Understand and use transition words and phrases
4	D	Choose a relevant topic sentence
5	C	Revise passages for organization

*Superlative phrases are formed by adding the word *most* in front of an adjective. The superlative adjective *commonest* can also be used, but the phrase "most commonest" is incorrect.

Q1. The student should list a word with the opposite meaning for each word. There is more than one correct antonym for each word. Sample answers are listed below.
- dark: light, fair, bright
- easy: hard, difficult
- cheap: costly, expensive, dear
- quiet: loud, noisy
- begin: end, finish
- neat: untidy, messy
- deep: shallow
- dry: wet, moist

Quiz 19

Question	Answer	Revising and Editing Skill
1	See Below	Identify adjectives and the noun they modify
2	B	Use irregular verbs correctly
3	B	Use correct subject-verb agreement
4	D	Understand and use transition words and phrases
5	B	Identify base words

Q1. The student should complete the table with any of the sets of adjectives and what the adjective is describing below:
- still, forest; dry, leaves; cool, night air; cold, air; humid, day; beautiful, night; lovely, song

Quiz 20

Question	Answer	Revising and Editing Skill
1	See Below	Identify adjectives used to compare things
2	C	Use correct punctuation (commas)
3	D	Edit sentences for correctness
4	A	Spell words correctly
5	D	Use correct capitalization

Q1. The student should complete each sentence with the examples below.

- The word *smallest* is used to compare Neptune to the other gas planets.
- The word *greater* is used to compare the radius of Neptune to the radius of Earth.

Section 2: Language, Vocabulary, and Grammar Quizzes

Quiz 21: Analyze Words
1. A
2. A
3. A
4. D

Quiz 22: Place Words in Alphabetical Order
1. A
2. B
3. B
4. B

Quiz 23: Divide Words into Syllables
1. car / pet
2. hope / ful
3. let / ter
4. no / tice
5. light / ing
6. hap / pen
7. farm / er
8. a / way
9. an / i / mal
10. im / por / tant
11. bas / ket / ball
12. but / ter / fly
13. ex / cite / ment
14. pas / sen/ ger

Quiz 24: Identify and Use Antonyms
1. C
2. A
3. B
4. A

Quiz 25: Identify Base Words
1. B
2. D
3. B
4. D

Quiz 26: Use Irregular Plurals

1. B
2. B
3. B
4. D

Quiz 27: Use Words with Suffixes

1. B
2. A
3. C
4. C

Quiz 28: Spell Commonly Misspelled Words

1. mother
2. house
3. school
4. welcome
5. pretty
6. decide

Quiz 29: Understand and Use Prefixes

1. B
2. B
3. A
4. B

Quiz 30: Understand and Use Suffixes

1. D
2. D
3. C
4. C

Quiz 31: Understand Greek and Latin Word Parts

1. A
2. C
3. A
4. C

Quiz 32: Spell Words with Suffixes Correctly
1. A
2. D
3. B
4. B

Quiz 33: Use Contractions
1. she's
2. we'll
3. they're
4. I've
5. he'd
6. couldn't

Quiz 34: Identify and Use Synonyms
1. B
2. A
3. D
4. A

Quiz 35: Identify Types of Words
1. C
2. C
3. A

Quiz 36: Use Verbs Correctly
1. D
2. B
3. A

Quiz 37: Use Correct Verb Tense
1. C
2. B
3. C
4. A

Quiz 38: Use Pronouns
1. C
2. A
3. B
4. D

Quiz 39: Use Possessive Pronouns

1. B
2. C
3. A
4. B

Quiz 40: Understand Word Meanings

1. D
2. B
3. C

Quiz 41: Spell Words Correctly

1. C
2. B
3. B
4. C

Quiz 42: Use Correct Punctuation

1. C
2. B
3. B
4. D

Quiz 43: Use Correct Capitalization

1. D
2. B
3. D
4. D

Quiz 44: Identify Base Words and Suffixes

1. save, ing
2. wait, ed
3. slap, ed
4. freeze, ing
5. glide, s
6. listen, er

Quiz 45: Use Homonyms and Homophones

1. B
2. C
3. B

Quiz 46: Use Homographs

Answers may vary. Sample answers are given below.

1. the sound a dog makes / part of a tree
2. to be healthy / a hole in the ground filled with water
3. a color / sad or upset
4. not weighing much / not dark in color
5. the outdoor area of a home / a unit of length

Quiz 47: Write Complete Sentences

1. A
2. A
3. A
4. B

Quiz 48: Use Coordinating Conjunctions

1. B
2. C
3. D

Texas Test Prep Practice Test Book

For focused reading test prep, get the Texas Test Prep Practice Test Book. It contains 8 reading mini-tests, focused vocabulary quizzes, plus a full-length STAAR Reading practice test.

Made in the USA
Charleston, SC
16 May 2014